Oscar Browning, William Harold Payne

A short History of Education

Oscar Browning, William Harold Payne

A short History of Education

ISBN/EAN: 9783337141318

Printed in Europe, USA, Canada, Australia, Japan

Cover: Foto ©ninafisch / pixelio.de

More available books at **www.hansebooks.com**

A SHORT
HISTORY OF EDUCATION

BEING A REPRINT OF THE ARTICLE BY OSCAR BROWNING ON

EDUCATION

IN THE NINTH EDITION OF THE

ENCYLOPÆDIA BRITANNICA

Edited, with an Introduction, Notes and References, and some account of
Comenius and his Writings,

BY

W. H. PAYNE, LL.D.

CHANCELLOR OF THE UNIVERSITY OF NASHVILLE. AUTHOR OF "CHAPTERS
ON SCHOOL SUPERVISION", "CONTRIBUTIONS TO THE SCIENCE
OF EDUCATION", ETC.

SYRACUSE, N. Y.
C. W. BARDEEN, PUBLISHER
1897

Copyright, 1881, by W. H. PAYNE; 1897, by C. W. BARDEEN

PUBLISHER'S NOTE

New plates being required for this little book, it has been thought best with the approval of the author to add illustrations, and accordingly thirty-six portraits and eleven other pictures have been inserted, with a few additional notes, mostly bibliographical.

SYRACUSE, *April* 16, 1897.

A SHORT

HISTORY OF EDUCATION

INTRODUCTION

In this country the purpose of normal instruction seems to be to prepare young men and women in the shortest and most direct way for doing school-room work. The equipment needed for this work is a knowledge of subjects and an empirical knowledge of methods; and so the normal schools furnish sound academic training, and pupils are taught methods of instruction by actual practice in experimental schools. In all this, the mechanical, or empirical, element seems to be held uppermost in thought. Pupils must be trained for practical ends; they must, so to speak, be converted into instruments for doing prescribed work by prescribed methods; and anything that promises to detract from their value as machines, must be studiously avoided. The artisan thus appears to be the ideal product of the normal school.

I do not presume to say that this conception of the purpose of normal instruction is wrong. I claim only the right to think and to say that I hold an essentially different view, and that I am attempting to give professional instruction to teachers on a totally different hypothesis. I believe that the great bar to educational progress is the mechanical teaching that is so prevalent, and that is so fostered and encouraged by normal schools. I believe that an intelligent scholar, furnished with a few clearly defined principles, and free to throw his own personality into his methods, is far more likely to grow into an accomplished teacher than one who goes to his work with the conviction that he must follow prescribed patterns, and has not that versatility that comes from an extension of his intellectual horizon. The value of a teacher depends upon his worth as a man, rather than upon his value as an instrument. Man becomes an instrument only by losing worth as a man. In normal instruction there is need of greater faith in the potency of ideas, and less faith in the value of drill, imitation, and routine.

It is possible that in some grades of school work a purely mechanical teaching is best; that he is the best teacher who is most of an artisan,—with whom teaching is most of a handicraft. But I do not believe this. The rules that are best for working on wood and stone are not the best when applied to mind and character. Undoubtedly, there is a mechanical element in the teaching art; but this is subordinate to that other element that wholly escapes mechanical measurements, because it has to do with the manifestations of free spirit. In other words, I am persuaded that a teacher is poor to the degree in which he is an artisan, and good to the degree in which he is an artist; and that nothing is so much needed by teachers of every class as an infusion of that freedom and versatility that are possible only through an extension of the mental vision by means of a more liberal culture.

While I may be wrong in the general hypothesis, I feel that I am right in the following particulars: There must be some teachers who are more than mere instruments, more than operatives, more than artisans; there must be some who can see processes as they are related to law,—who, while obedient to law, can throw their own personality into their methods and can make such adaptations of them as varying circumstances may demand. If most teachers are doomed to be the slaves of routine, there must be some who have the ability to create and to control. In a word, along with the great multitude of mere teachers, there must be a growing body of educators. I cannot but think that in every normal school there are men and women who would love to walk upon these heights, to breathe this freer air, and who would thus see in teaching a fair field for the exercise of their best gifts. The attention of such should be drawn somewhat away from the merely mechanical aspects of teaching, and fixed on those professional studies that will broaden the teacher's vision and give him the consciousness of some degree of creative power. The studies I mean are EDUCATIONAL SCIENCE and EDUCATIONAL HISTORY.

It has been said that a teacher who is wholly ignorant of the history of education may still do excellent work in the school-room. This does not admit of the least doubt. It is also true that men attain long lives in complete ignorance of the laws of digestion, and that they become voters and officeholders while knowing nothing of their country's history; but it does not follow that physiology and history are needless studies. A fair knowledge of the history of one's own country is now thought to be an essential element in good citizenship; and I see no reason why a fair knowledge of the history of educational systems and doctrines should not form a very desirable element in a teacher's education. He may teach well without this knowledge; but having it, he will feel an inspiring sense of the nobility of his calling, will teach more intelligently, and will give a richer quality to his work. Intelligent patriotism is evoked by a vivid knowledge of Plymouth Rock, of the American Revolution, and of Mount Vernon; and no teacher can think meanly of his calling who has learned to trace his professional ancestry through Plato, Comenius, Locke, Cousin, and Arnold.

As exhibiting the general grounds on which the history of education should be made a topic of instruction for at least a part of the teaching class, I repeat some observations made on another occasion.

"General history is a liberal study in the sense that it greatly extends the horizon of our sympathies, widens our field of intellectual vision, and thus makes us cosmopolitan and catholic,—true citizens of the world. Historical study has also a very great practical value. It gives us the benefit of collective human experience as exhibited under every variety of circumstances and conditions. It relates the origin, succession, and termination of all the marked events in human progress. It thus saves us from repeating experiments already tried, forewarns us against dangers that ever beset the path of the inexperienced, and assures to each generation the results of the real additions made to the stock of human progress.

"For the most part, the events recorded in history are the results of the unpremeditated actions of man **Humanity at** large seems to be impelled onward by an irresistible but unconscious impulse, just as a glacier moves over mountains and through valleys, with a silent yet irresistible might. This life of mere impulse is the lower life of nations and peoples, just as the period of impulse marks the lower and imperfect life of the individual. But in **nations as** well as in individuals, the **period of** reflection at **last** comes, and this is the period when histories begin to be written and read. The effect of historical study **is thus to check** mere impulse, and to convert uncon**scious** progress into self-conscious and reflective efforts towards determinate ends.

"In all nations that have passed beyond the period of mere barbarism, there has been some degree of conscious and intended effort after progress, some preparation for the duties of citizenship, some attempt to make the **future** better than the past has been. This conscious effort to place **each** generation on a vantage-ground, through some deliberate **training or** preparation, is, in its widest **sense,** education.

"**Now if** history in general, as it records the unconscious phases of human progress, is a study of supreme value, that **part of** general history which records the reflective efforts **of men to rise** superior to their actual present, must teach **lessons of** even higher **value.** This is emphatically **an** educating age. The minds of the wisest and the best are intent on devising means whereby progress may be hastened through the resources of human art. In the world of educational thought, all is ferment and discussion. We are passing beyond the period of reckless experiment and are seeking anchorage in doctrines deduced from the permanent principles of human nature. Educational Science is giving us a glimmer of light ahead, and we do well to shape our course by it. *What ought to be* should indeed be our pole-star; but until this has been defined with more precision, we should also shape our course by looking back on *what has been*. We should think of ourselves as moving through the darkness or over an unknown region, with a light before us and a light behind us. Our two inquiries should be, Whence have we come? Whither are we going? Historical progress is tortuous, but its general direction is right. The history of what has been must therefore contain some elements of truth. The past at least foreshadows the future, and we may infer the direction of progress by comparing *what has been* with *what is*. In education, therefore, we need to know the past, both as a means of taking stock of progress, and also of foreshadowing the future. We should give a large place to the ideal elements in our courses of normal instruction; but we should also make a large use of the results of experience. All true progress is a transition. The past has insensibly led up to the present; let the present merge into the future. Let history foreshadow philosophy; and let philosophy introduce its corrections and ameliorations into the lessons of history."

An obstacle to the study of the history of education in this country, has been the lack of suitable books on this subject. In English we have only Schmidt's *History of Education,* and the *History and Progress of Education* by Philobiblius (L. P. Brockett). At best, these are mere outlines, and considered as outlines, they are very imperfect and unsatisfactory. In seeking for a text that I might make the basis of a short course of instruction for students in this university, I have found the article EDUCATION in the ninth edition of the Encyclopædia Britannica admirably adapted to my purpose; and I have thought that a reprint of it, under the title of *A Short History of Education* might be acceptable to the general reader, to intelligent and progressive teachers, and to the members of the profession who are engaged in the education of teachers. To make this outline more useful to teachers and students, I have added a select list of educational works, and have arranged a list of more important topics suggested by this outline, with references to these authorities. By this means the course of study may be extended almost at will. It may be embraced merely this admirable outline, and thus occupy but a few days, or it may be pursued on the seminary plan, and thus indefinitely extended. I have considerably multiplied my notes and references on Comenius, in the hope of exciting an interest in the study of one of the greatest of the educational reformers.

W. H. PAYNE

UNIVERSITY OF MICHIGAN, *January* 22, 1881.

A Short History of Education

This article is mainly concerned with the history of educational theories in the chief crises of their development. It has not been the object of the writer to give a history of the practical working of these theories, and still less to sketch the outlines of the science of teaching, which may be more conveniently dealt with under another head.

The earliest education is that of the family. The child must be trained not to interfere with its parents' convenience, and to acquire those little arts which will help in maintaining the economy of the household. It was long before any attempt was made to improve generations as they succeeded each other.

The earliest schools were those of the priests. As soon as an educated priesthood had taken the place of the diviners and jugglers who abused the credulity of the earliest races, schools of the prophets became a necessity. The training required for ceremonials, the common life apart from the family, the accomplishments of reading and singing, afforded a nucleus for the organization of culture and an opportunity for the efforts of a philosopher in advance of his age. Convenience and gratitude confirmed the monopoly of the clergy.

The schools of Judea and Egypt were ecclesiastical. The Jews had but little effect on the progress of science, but our obligations to the priests of the Nile valley are great indeed. Much of their learning is obscure to us, but we have reason to conclude that there is no branch of science in which they did not progress at least so far as observation and careful registration of facts could carry them. They were a source of enlightenment to surrounding nations. Not only the great lawgiver of the Jews, but those who were most active in stimulating the nascent energies of Hellas were careful to train themselves in the wisdom of the Egyptians.

Greece, in giving an undying name to the literature of Alexander, was only repaying the debt which she had incurred centuries before. Education became secular in countries where the priesthood did not exist as a separate body. At Rome, until Greece took her conqueror captive, a child was trained for the duties of life in the forum and the senate house.

ARISTOTLE, 384-332, B. C.

The Greeks were the first to develop a science of education distinct from ecclesiastical training. They divided their subjects of study into music and gymnastics, the one comprising all mental, the other all physical training. Music was at first little more than the study of the art of expression.

But the range of intellectual education which had been developed by distinguished musical teachers was further widened by the Sophists, until it received a new stimulus and direction from the work of Socrates. Who can forget the picture left us by Plato of the Athenian palæstra, in which Socrates was sure to find his most ready listeners and his most ardent disciples? In the intervals of running, wrestling, or the bath, the young Phædrus or Theætetus discoursed with the philosophers who had come to watch them on the good, the beautiful, and the true. The lowest efforts of their teachers were to fit them to maintain any view they might adopt with acuteness, elegance, readiness, and good taste. Their highest efforts were to stimulate a craving for the knowledge of the unknowable, to rouse a dissatisfaction with received opinions, and to excite a curiosity which grew stronger with the revelation of each successive mystery.

SOCRATES, 470-399, B. C.

Plato is the author of the first systematic treatise on education. He deals with the subject in his earlier dialogues, he enters into it with great fulness of detail in the *Republic*, and it occupies an important position in the *Laws*. The views thus expressed differ considerably in particulars, and it is therefore difficult to give concisely the precepts drawn up by him for our obedience. But the same spirit under lies his whole teaching. He never forgets that the beautiful is undistinguishable from the true, and that the mind is best fitted to solve difficult problems which has been trained by the enthusiastic contemplation of art.

Plato proposes to intrust education to the state.

PLATO, 429-347, B. C.

He lays great stress on the influence of race and blood. Strong and worthy children are likely to spring from strong and worthy parents. Music and gymnastics are to develop the emotions of young men during their earliest years—the one to strengthen their character for the contest of life, the other to excite in them varying feelings of resentment or tenderness. Reverence, the ornament of youth, is to be called forth by well-chosen fictions; a long and rigid training in science is to precede discussion on more important subjects. At length the goal is reached, and the ripest wisdom is ready to be applied to the most important practice.

The great work of Quintilian, although mainly a treatise on oratory, also contains incidentally a complete sketch of a theoretical education. His object is to show us how to form the man of practice. But what a high conception of practice is his! He wrote for a race of rulers. He inculcates much which has been attributed to the wisdom of a later age. He urges the importance of studying individual dispositions, and of tenderness in discipline and punishment.

The Romans understood no systematic training except in oratory. In their eyes every citizen was a born commander, and they knew of no science of government and political economy. Cicero speaks slightingly even of jurisprudence. Any one, he says, can make himself a jurisconsult in a week, but an orator is the production of a lifetime. No statement can be less true than that a perfect orator is a perfect man. But wisdom and philanthrophy broke even through that barrier, and the training which Quintilian expounds to us as intended only for the public speaker would, in the language of Milton, fit a man to perform justly, wisely, and magnanimously all the offices, both public and private, of peace and war.

Such are the ideas which the old world has left us. On one side man, beautiful, active, clever, receptive, emotional, quick to feel, to show his feeling, to argue, to refine; greedy of the pleasures of the world, perhaps a little neglectful of its duties, fearing restraint as an unjust stinting of the bounty of nature, inquiring eagerly into every secret, strongly attached to the things of this life, but elevated by an unabated striving after the highest ideal; setting no value but upon faultless abstractions, and seeing reality only in heaven, on earth mere shadows, phantoms, and copies of the unseen. On the other side, man, practical, energetic, eloquent, tinged but not imbued with philosophy, trained to spare neither himself nor others, reading and thinking only with an apology; best engaged in defending a political principle, in maintaining with gravity and solemnity the conservation of ancient freedom, in leading armies through unexplored deserts, establishing roads, fortresses, settlements, the results of conquest, or in ordering and superintending the slow, certain, and utter annihilation of some enemy of Rome. Has the modern world ever surpassed their type? Can we in the present day produce anything by education except by combining, blending, and modifying the self-culture of the Greek or the self-sacrifice of the Roman?

The literary education of the earliest generation of Christians was obtained in the pagan schools, in those great imperial academies which existed even down to the fifth century, which flourished in Europe, Asia, and Africa, and attained perhaps their highest development and efficiency in Gaul.

The first attempt to provide a special education for Christians was made at Alexandria, and is illustrated by the names of Clement and Origen. The later Latin fathers took a bolder stand, and rejected the suspicious aid of heathenism. Tertullian, Cyprian, and Jerome wished the antagonism between Christianity and Paganism to be recognized from the earliest years, and even Augustine condemned with harshness the culture to which he owed so much of his influence.

The education of the Middle Ages was either that of the cloister or the castle. They stood in sharp contrast to each other. The object of the one was to form the young monk, of the other the young knight. We should indeed be ungrateful if we forgot the services of those illustrious monasteries, Monte Cassino, Fulda, or Tours, which kept alive the torch of learning throughout the dark ages, but it would be equally mistaken to attach an exaggerated importance to the teachings which they provided. Long hours were spent in the duties of the church and in learning to take a part in elaborate and useless ceremonies. A most important part of the monastery was the writing-room, where missals, psalters, and breviaries were copied and illuminated, and too often a masterpiece of classic literature was effaced to make room for a treatise of one of the fathers or the sermon of an abbot.

The discipline was hard; the rod ruled all with indiscriminating and impartial severity. How many generations have had to suffer for the floggings of those times! Hatred of learning, antagonism between the teacher and the taught, the belief that no training can be effectual which is not repulsive and distasteful, that no subject is proper for instruction which is acquired with ease and pleasure—all these idols of false education have their root and origin in monkish cruelty. The joy of human life would have been in danger of being stamped out if it had not been for the warmth and color of a young knight's boyhood. He was equally well broken in to obedience and hardship; but the obedience was the willing service of a mistress whom he loved, and the hardship the permission to share the dangers of a leader whom he emulated.

The seven arts of monkish training were Grammar, Dialectics, Rhetoric, Music, Arithmetic, Geometry, Astronomy, which together formed the *trivium* and *quadrivium*, the seven years' course, the divisions of which have profoundly affected our modern training.

One of the earliest treatises based on this method was that of Martianus Capella, who in 470 published his *Satyra*, in nine books. The first two were devoted to the marriage between Philology and Mercury; the last seven were each devoted to the consideration of one of these liberal arts. Cassiodorus, who wrote *De Septem Disciplinis* about 500, was also largely used as a text-book in the schools. Astronomy was taught by the Cisio-Janus, a collection of doggrel hexameters like the *Propria quæ maribus*, which contained the chief festivals in each month, with a *memoria technica* for recollecting when they occurred.

The seven knightly accomplishments, as historians tell us, were to ride, to swim, to shoot with the bow, to box, to hawk, to play chess, and to make verses. The verses thus made were not in Latin, bald imitations of Ovid or Horace, whose pagan beauties were wrested into the service of religion, but sonnets, ballads, and canzonets in soft Provençal or melodious Italian.

In nothing, perhaps, is the difference between these two forms of education more clearly shown than in their relations to women. A young monk was brought up to regard a woman as the worst among the many temptations of St. Anthony. His life knew no domestic tenderness or affection. He was surrounded and cared for by celibates, to be himself a celibate. A page was trained to receive his best reward and worst punishment from the smile or frown of the lady of the castle, and as he grew to manhood to cherish an absorbing passion as the strongest stimulus to a noble life, and the contemplation of female virtue, as embodied in an Isolde or a Beatrice, as the truest earnest of future immortality.

Both these forms of education disappeared before the Renaissance and the Reformation. But we must not suppose that no efforts were made to improve upon the narrowness of the schoolmen or the idleness of chivalry. The schools of Charles the Great have lately been investigated by Mr. Mullinger, but we do not find that they materially advanced the science of education. Vincent of Beauvais has left us a very complete treatise on education, written about the year 1245. He was the friend and counsellor of St. Louis, and we may discern his influence in the instructions which were left by that sainted king for the guidance of his son and daughter through life.

The end of this period was marked by the rise of universities. Bologna devoted itself to law, and numbered 12,000 students at the end of the 12th century. Salerno adopted as its special province the study of medicine, and Paris was thronged with students from all parts of Europe, who were anxious to devote themselves to a theology which passed by indefinite gradations into philosophy. The 14th and 15th centuries witnessed the rise of universities and academies in almost every portion of Europe.

Perhaps the most interesting among these precursors of a higher culture were the Brethren of the Common Life, who were domiciled in the rich meadows of the Yssel, in the Northern Netherlands. The metropolis of their organization was Deventer, the best known name among them that of Gerhard Groote. They devoted themselves with all humility and self-sacrifice to the education of children. Their schools were crowded. Bois-le-Duc numbered 1200 pupils, Zwolle 1500. For a hundred years no part of Europe shone with a brighter lustre.

As the divine comedy of Dante represents for us the learning and piety of the Middle Ages in Italy, so the *Imitation* of Thomas a Kempis keeps alive for us the memory of the purity and sweetness of the Dutch community. But they had not sufficient strength to preserve their supremacy among the necessary developments of the age. They could not support the glare of the new Italian learning; they obtained, and it may be feared deserved, the title of obscurantists. The *Epistolæ Obscurorum Virorum*, the wittiest squib of the Middle Ages, which was so true and so subtle in its satire that it was hailed as a blow struck in defence of the ancient learning, consists in great part of the lamentations of the brethren of Deventer over the new age, which they could not either comprehend or withstand.

The education of the Renaissance is best represented by the name of Erasmus, that of the Reformation by the names of Luther and Melanchthon. We have no space to give an account of that marvellous resurrection of the mind and spirit of Europe when touched by the dead hand of an extinct civilization. The history of the revival of letters belongs rather to the general history of literature than to that of education. But there are two names whom we ought not to pass over.

Vittorino da Feltre was summoned by the Gonzagas to Mantua in 1424; he was lodged in a spacious palace, with galleries, halls, and colonnades decorated with frescoes of playing children. In person he was small, quick, and lively—a born schoolmaster, whose whole time was spent in devotion to his pupils. We are told of the children of his patron, how Prince Gonzaga recited 200 verses of his own composition at the age of fourteen, and how Prince Cecilia wrote elegant Greek at the age of ten. Vittorino died in 1477. He seems to have reached the highest point of excellence as a practical schoolmaster of the Italian Renaissance.

Castiglione, on the other hand has left us in his *Cortigiano* the sketch of a cultivated nobleman in those most cultivated days. He shows by what precepts and practice the golden youths of Verona and Venice were formed, who live for us in the plays of Shakespeare as models of knightly excellence.

For our instruction, it is better to have recourse to the pages of Erasmus. He has written the most minute account of his method of teaching. The child is to be formed into a good Greek and Latin scholar and a pious man. He fully grasps the truth that improvement must be natural and gradual. Letters are to be taught playing. The rules of grammar are to be few and

ERASMUS, 1467-1536

short. Every means of arousing interest in the work is to be fully employed. Erasmus is no Ciceronian. Latin is to be taught so as to be of use—a living language adapted to modern wants. Children should learn an art—painting, sculpture, or architecture. Idleness is above all things to be avoided. The education of girls is as necessary and important as that of boys. Much depends upon home influence; obedience must be strict, but not too severe. We must take account of individual peculiarities, and not force children into cloisters against their will. We shall obtain the best result by following nature.

It is easy to see what a contrast this scheme presented to the monkish training,—to the routine of useless technicalities enforced amidst the shouts of teachers and the lamentations of the taught.

Still this culture was but for the few. Luther brought the schoolmaster into the cottage, and laid the foundations of the system which is the chief honor and strength of modern Germany, a system by which the child of the humblest peasant, by slow but certain gradations, receives the best education which the country can afford. The precepts of Luther found their way into the hearts of his countrymen in short, pithy sentences, like the sayings of Poor Richard. The purification and widen-

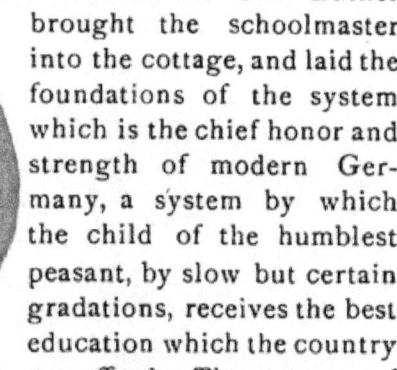

MARTIN LUTHER, 1483-1546

ing of education went hand in hand with the purification of religion, and these claims to affection are indissolubly united in the minds of his countrymen.

Melanchthon, from his editions of school books and his practical labors in education, earned the title of Præceptor Germanæ. Aristotle had been dethroned from his pre-eminence in the schools, and Melanchthon attempted to supply his place. He appreciated the importance of Greek, the terror of the obscurantists, and is the author of a Greek grammar. He wrote elementary books on each department of the *trivium*—grammar, dialect, and rhetoric. He made some way with the studies of the *quadrivium*, and wrote *Initia doctrinæ Physicæ*, a primer of physical science. He lectured at the university of Wittenberg, and for ten years, from 1519 to 1529, kept a *schola privata* in his own house.

PHILIPP MELANCHTHON,
1497-1560

Horace was his favorite classic. His pupils were taught to learn the whole of it by heart, ten lines at a time. The tender refined lines of his well-known portraits show clearly the character of the painful, accurate scholar, and contrast with the burly powerful form of the genial Luther He died in 1560, racked with anxiety for the church which he had helped to found. If he did not carry Protestantism into the heart of the peasant, he at least made it acceptable to the intellect of the man of letters.

We now come to the names of three theoretical and practical teachers who have exercised and are still exercising a profound effect over education. The so-called Latin school, the parent of the gymnasium and the lycee, had spread all over Europe, and was especially flourishing in Germany. The programmes and time tables in use in these establishments have come down to us, and we possess notices of the lives and labors of many of the earliest teachers. It is not difficult to trace a picture of the education which the Reformation offered to the middle classes of Europe. Ample material exists in German histories of education. We must confine ourselves to those moments which were of vital influence in the development of the science.

One school stands pre-eminently before the rest, situated in that border city on the debatable land between France and Germany, which has known how to combine and reconcile the peculiarities of French and German culture. Strasburg, besides a school of theology which unites the depth of Germany to the clearness and vivacity of France, educated the gilded youth of the 16th century under Sturm, as it trained the statesmen and diplomatists of the 18th under Koch. John Sturm

JOHN STURM, 1507-1589

ROGER ASCHAM AND LADY JANE GREY

of Strasburg was the friend of Ascham, the author of the *Scholemaster*, and the tutor of Queen Elizabeth. It was Ascham who found Lady Jane Grey alone in her room at Bradgate bending her neck over the page of Plato when all the rest of her family were following the chase.

Sturm was the first great head-master, the progenitor of Busbys if not of Arnolds. He lived and worked till the age of eighty-two. He was a friend of all the most distinguished men of his age, the chosen representative of the Protestant cause in Europe, the ambassador to foreign powers. He was believed to be better informed than any man of his time of the complications of foreign politics. Rarely did an envoy pass from France to Germany without turning aside to profit by his experience.

THOMAS ARNOLD, 1795-1842

But the chief energies of his life were devoted to teaching. He drew his scholars from the whole of Europe; Portugal, Poland, England sent their contingent to his halls. In 1578, his school numbered several thousand students; he supplied at once the place of the cloister and the castle. What he most insisted upon was the teaching of Latin, not the conversational *lingua franca* of Erasmus, but pure, elegant Ciceronian Latinity. He may be called the introducer of scholarship into the schools, a scholarship which as yet took little account of Greek. His pupils would write elegant letters, deliver elegant Latin speeches, be familiar, if not with the thoughts, at least with the language of the ancients, would be scholars in order that they might be gentlemen.

Our space will not permit us to trace the whole course of his influence, but he is in all probability as much answerable as any one for the euphuistic refinement which overspread Europe in the 16th century, and which went far to ruin and corrupt its literatures. Nowhere perhaps had he more effect than in England. Our older public schools, on breaking with the ancient faith, looked to Sturm as their model of Protestant education. His name and example became familiar to us by the exertions of his friend Ascham. Westminster, under the long reign of Busby, received a form which was generally accepted as the type of a gentleman's education. The Public School Commission of 1862 found that the lines laid down by the great citizen of Strasburg, and copied by his admirers, had remained unchanged until within the memory of the present generation.

Wolfgang Ratke or Ratichius was born in Holstein in 1571. He anticipated some of the best improvements in the method of teaching which have been made in modern times. He was like many of those who have tried to improve existing methods in advance of his age, and he was rewarded for his labors at Augsburg, Weimar, and Köthen by persecution and imprisonment. Can we wonder that education has improved so slowly when so much pains has been taken to silence and extinguish those who have devoted themselves to its improvement?

His chief rules were as follows:

1. Begin everything with prayer.
2. Do everything in order, following the course of nature.
3. One thing at a time.
4. Often repeat the same thing.
5. Teach everything first in the mother tongue.
6. Proceed from the mother tongue to other languages.
7. Teach without compulsion. Do not beat children to make them learn. Pupils must love their masters, not hate them. Nothing should be learnt by heart. Sufficient time should be given to play and recreation. Learn one thing before going on to another. Do not teach for two hours consecutively.
8. Uniformity in teaching, also in school-books, especially grammars, which may with advantage be made comparative.
9. Teach a thing first, and then the reason of it. Give no rules before you have given the examples. Teach no language out of the grammar, but out of authors.
10. Let everything be taught by induction and experiment.

Most of these precepts are accepted by all good teachers in the present day; all of them are full of wisdom. Unfortunately their author saw the faults of the teaching of his time more clearly than the means to remove them, and he was more successful in forming precepts than in carrying them out. Notwithstanding these drawbacks, he deserves an honorable place among the forerunners of a rational education.

John Amos Comenius was the antithesis to Sturm, and a greater man than Ratke. Born a Moravian, he passed a wandering life, among the troubles of the Thirty Years' War, in poverty and obscurity. But his ideas were accepted by the most advanced thinkers of the age, notably in many respects by our own Milton, and by Oxenstiern, the chancellor of Sweden. His school books were spread throughout Europe. The *Janua Linguarum Reservata* was translated into twelve European and several Asiatic languages. His works, especially the *Didascalia magna*, an encyclopædia of the science of education, are constantly reprinted at the present day; and the system which he sketched will be found to foreshadow the education of the future.

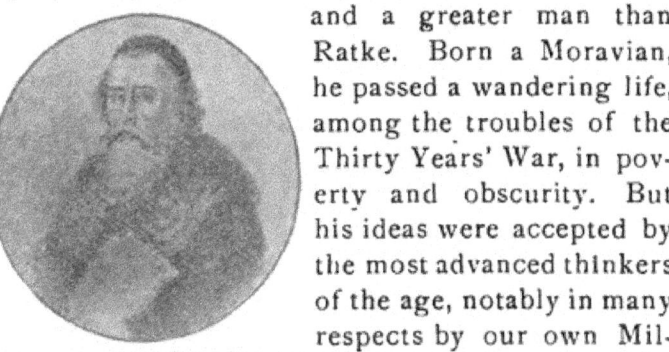

JOHN AMOS COMENIUS, 1592-1671

He was repelled and disgusted by the long delays and pedantries of the schools. His ardent mind conceived that if teachers would but follow nature instead of forcing it against its bent, take full advantage of the innate desire for activity and growth, all men might be able to learn all things. Languages should be taught as the mother tongue is taught, by conversations on ordinary topics; pictures, object lessons should be freely used; teaching should go hand in hand with a cheerful elegant, and happy life. Comenius included in his course the teaching of the mother tongue, singing, economy, and politics, the history of the world, physical geography, and a knowledge of arts and handicrafts.

JANUA LINGUARUM RESERATA:

SIVE,

Omnium Scientiarum & Linguarum SEMINARIUM:

ID EST,

Compendiosa Latinam & Anglicam, aliasque Linguas & Artium etiam fundamenta addiscendi methodu; unà cum Januæ Latinitatis Vestibulo.

Autore Cl. Viro J. A. COMENIO.

The GATE of LANGUAGES UNLOCKED:

Or, a SEED-PLOT of all Arts and Tongues; containing a ready way to learn the Latine and English Tongue.

Formerly translated by THO. HORN: afterwards much corrected and amended by JOH. ROBOTHAM: now carefully reviewed by W. D. to which is premised a PORTAL.

As also, there is now newly added the Foundation to the *Janua*, containing all or the chiefe Primitives of the Latine Tongue, drawn into Sentences, in an Alphabeticall order by G. P.

LONDON,

Printed by *Edw. Griffin*, and *Wil. Hunt*, for *Thomas Slater*, and are to be sold by the Company of Stationers. 1652.

Quatuor Evangelistæ, quinque sensus, sex profesti dies.	Four Evangelists, five senses, six "working dayes.	"Not hallowed.
Septem petitiones in Oratione Dominica.	"Seven petitions in the Lord's Prayer.	"So the L. Bishop of Landaff in his Treatise of the Sacrament of the Lords Supper divides them.
Octo dies sunt septimana.	Eight dayes are a week.	
Ter tria sunt novem.	Thrice three are nine.	
Decem precepta Dei.	Ten Commandements of God.	
Undecim Apostoli, dempto Juda.	Eleven Apostles, Judas being excepted.	
Duodecim fidei articuli.	Twelve Articles of the Faith.	
Triginta dies sunt mensis.	Thirty dayes are a moneth.	
Centum anni sunt seculum.	A hundred years are an age.	
Satanas est mille fraudum artifex.	Satan is the forger of a thousand deceits.	

CAP. 4.
De rebus in schola

CHAP. 4.
Of things in a school.

Scholasticus frequentat scholam.	A Scholar frequenteth the schoole.
Quò in artibus erudiatur.	That he may be instructed in the arts.
Initium est à literis.	The begining is from letters.
E syllabis voces componuntur	Words are composed of syllables.
E dictionibus sermo.	A speech of words.
Ex libro legimus tacitè.	We read silently out of a book.
Aut recitamus clarè.	Or recite it aloud.
Involvimus eum membranâ	We wrap it up in parchment.
Et ponimus in pulpito.	And lay it in a desk.
Atramentum est in atramentario, in quo tingimus calamum	Ink is in the ink-horn, in which we dip the quill.
Scribimus eo in charta, in utraque pagina.	We write with it in paper, on either page.
Si perperam, delemus.	If badly, we blot it out.
Et signamus denuo rectè, vel in margine.	And then mark it in the line, or in the margent.
Doctor docet.	A teacher teacheth.
Discipulus discit non omnia simul, sed per partes.	A scholar learneth not altogether, but by parts.
Præceptor præcipit facienda.	The Master commands things to be done.
Rector regit Academiam	The Governor ruleth the Academie

But the principle on which he most insisted, which forms the special point of his teaching, and in which he is followed by Milton, is that the teaching of words and things must go together hand in hand. When we consider how much time is spent over new languages, what waste of energy is lavished on mere preparation, how it takes so long to lay a foundation that there is no time to rear a building upon it, we must conclude that it is in the acceptance and development of this principle that the improvement of education will in the future consist. Any one who attempts to inculcate this great reform will find that its first principles are contained in the writings of Comenius.

But this is not the whole of his claim upon our gratitude. He was one of the first advocates of the teaching of science in schools. His kindness, gentleness, and sympathy make him the forerunner of Pestalozzi. His general principles of education would not sound strange in the treatise of Herbert Spencer.

The Protestant schools were now the best in Europe, and the monkish institutions were left to decay. Catholics would have remained behind in the race if it had not been for the Jesuits. Ignatius Loyola gave this direction to the order which he founded, and the programme of studies, which dates from the end of the sixteenth century, is in

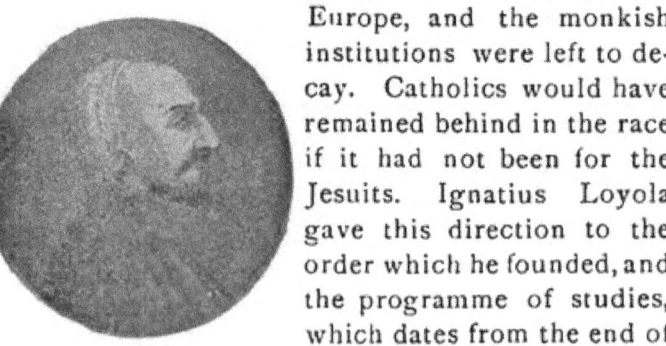

IGNATIUS DE LOYOLA, 1491-1556

use, with certain modifications, in English Jesuit schools at the present day. In 1550 the first Jesuit school was opened in Germany; in 1700 the order possessed 612 colleges, 157 normal schools, 59 noviciates, 340 residences, 200 missions, 29 professed homes, and 24 universities. The college of Clermont had 3000 students in 1695.

Every Jesuit college was divided into two parts, the one for higher, the other for lower education,—the *studia superiora* and the *studia inferiora*. The *studia inferiora*, answering to the modern gymnasium, was divided into five classes. The first three were classes of grammar (rudiments), grammar (accidence), and syntax; the last two humanity and rhetoric.

The motto of the schools was *lege, scribe, loquere,*—you must learn not only to read and write a dead language, but to talk. Purism was even more exaggerated that by Sturm. No word might be used which did not rest upon a special authority. The composition of Latin verses was strongly encouraged, and the performance of Latin plays. Greek was studied to some extent; mathematics, geography, music, and the mother tongues were neglected.

The *studia superiora* began with a philosophical course of two or three years. In the first year logic was taught, in the second the books of Aristotle, *de cælo*, the first book *de generatione*, and the *Meteorologica*. In the third year the second book *de generatione*, the books *de anima*, and the *Metaphysics*. After the completion of the philosophical course the pupil studied theology for four years.

The Jesuits used to the full the great engine of emulation. Their classes were divided into two parts, Romans and Carthaginians; swords, shields, and lances hung on the walls, and were carried off in triumph as either party claimed the victory by a fortunate answer.

It would be unfair to deny the merits of the education of the Jesuits. Bacon speaks of them in more than one passage as the revivers of this most important art. *Quum talis sis utinam noster esses.* Descartes approved of their system; Chateaubriand regarded their suppression as a calamity to civilization and enlightenment. They were probably the first to bring the teacher into close connection with the taught. According to their ideal the teacher was neither inclosed in a cloister, secluded from his pupils, nor did he keep order by stamping, raving, and flogging. He was encouraged to apply his mind and soul to the mind and soul of his pupil; to study the nature, the disposition, the parents of his scholars; to follow nature as far as possible, or rather to lie in wait for it and discover its weak points, and where it could be most easily

FRANCIS BACON, 1561-1626

RENÉ DESCARTES, 1596-1650

attacked. Doubtless the Jesuits have shown a love, devotion, and self-sacrifice in education, which is worthy of the highest praise; no teacher who would compete with them can dare do less.

On the other hand, they are open to grave accusation. Their watchful care degenerated into surveillance, which lay-schools have borrowed from them; their study of nature has led them to confession and direction. They have tracked out the soul to its recesses, that they might slay it there, and generate another in its place; they educated each mind according to its powers, that it might be a more subservient tool to their own purposes. They taught the accomplishments which the world loves, but their chief object was to amuse the mind and stifle inquiry; they engaged Latin verses, because they were a convenient plaything on which powers might be exercised which could have been better employed in understanding and discussing higher subjects; they were the patrons of school plays, of public prizes, declamations, examinations, and other exhibitions, in which the parents were more considered than the boys; they regarded the claims of education, not as a desire to be encouraged, but as a demand to be played with and propitiated; they gave the best education of their time in order to acquire confidence, but they became the chief obstacle to the improvement, of education; they did not care for enlightenment, but only for the influence which they could derive from a supposed regard for enlightenment.

What may have been the service of Jesuits in past times, we have little to hope for them in the improvement of education at present. Governments have, on the whole, acted wisely by checking and suppressing their colleges. The *ratio studiorum* is antiquated and difficult to reform. In 1831 it was brought more into accordance with modern ideas by Roothaan, the general of the order. Beckx, his successor, has, if anything, pursued a policy of retrogression. The Italian Government, in taking possession of Rome, found that the pupils of the Collegio Romano were far below the level of modern requirements.

It may be imagined that, by this organization both Catholic and Protestant were apt to degenerate into pedantry, both in name and purpose. The schoolmaster had a great deal too much the best of it. The Latin school was tabulated and organized until every half hour of a boy's time was occupied; the Jesuit school took possession of the pupil body and soul. It was, therefore, to be expected that a stand should be made for common sense in the direction of practice rather than theory, of wisdom instead of learning.

Montaigne has left us the most delightful utterances about education. He says that the faults of the education of his day consist in overestimating the intellect and rejecting morality, in exaggerating memory and depreciating useful knowledge. He recommends a tutor who should draw out the pupil's own power and originality, to teach how to live well and to die well, to enforce a lesson by practice, to put

MICHEL EQUEM DE MONTAIGNE, 1533-1592

the mother tongue before foreign tongues, to teach all manly exercises, to educate the perfect man. Away with force and compulsion, with severity and the rod.

John Locke, more than a hundred years afterwards, made a more powerful and systematic attack upon useless knowledge. His theory of the origin of ideas led him to assign great importance to education, while his knowledge of the operations of the human mind lends a special value to his advice. His treatise has received in England more attention than it deserves, partly because we have so few books written upon the subject on which he treats Part of his advice is useless at the present day; part it would be well to follow, or at any rate to consider seriously, especially his condemnation of repetition by heart as a means of strengthening the memory, and of Latin verses and themes.

JOHN LOCKE, 1632-1704

He sets before himself the production of the man, a sound mind in a sound body. His knowledge of medicine gives great value to his advice on the earliest education, although he probably exaggerates the benefits of enforced hardships. He recommends home education without harshness or severity of discipline. Emulation is to be the chief spring of action; knowledge is far less valuable than a well-trained mind. He prizes that knowledge most which fits a man for the duties of the world, speaking languages, accounts, history, law, logic, rhetoric, natural philosophy. He inculcates the importance of drawing, dancing, riding, fencing, and trades.

The part of his advice which made the most impression upon his contemporaries was the teaching of reading and arithmetic by well-considered games, the discouragement of an undue compulsion and punishment, and the teaching of language without the drudgery of grammar. In these respects he has undoubtedly anticipated modern discoveries. He is a strong advocate for home education under a private tutor, and his bitterness against public schools is as vehement as that of Cowper.

Far more important in the literature of this subject than the treatise of Locke is the *Tractate of Education** by Milton, "the few observations," as he tells us, "which flowered off, and are, as it were, the burnishings of many studious and contemplative years spent in search for civil and religious knowledge." This essay is addressed to Samuel Hartlib, a great friend of Comenius, and probably refers to a project of establishing a university in London.

JOHN MILTON, 1608-1674

"I will point you out," Milton says, "the right path of a virtuous and noble education,—laborious, indeed,

---

*School Room Classics, vi. A Small Tractate of Education, by John Milton, 16:26, 15 cts. Syracuse, N. Y., C. W. Bardeen.

at first ascent, but else so smooth and green and full of goodly prospects and melodious sounds on every side, that the harp of Orpheus is not more charming." This is to be done between twelve and one-and-twenty, in an academy containing about a hundred and thirty scholars, which shall be at once **school** and **university**,—not **needing a remove to any** other house of scholarship **except** it be some peculiar college of law **and** physics, where they mean to be practitioners.

The important truth enunciated **is quite in the** spirit of Comenius **that the learning of things and words is to go hand in** hand. The curriculum **is very large.** Latin, Greek, arithmetic, geometry, agriculture, geography, physiology, physics, **trigonometry,** fortification, architecture, engineering, navigation, anatomy, medicine, poetry, **Italian, law,** both **Roman and** English, Hebrew, with Chaldee and **Syriac,** history, oratory, poetics.

But the scholars are not to be book-**worms.** They **are to be trained for war,** both **on** foot and **on** horseback, to be practised "**in all the** locks and **gripes** of **wrestling," they are to "recreate** and compose their **travailed spirits with the divine** harmonies of music heard or **learnt." "In those** vernal seasons **of the year when the air is calm and pleasant,** it **were an injury** and **a sullenness against** Nature **not to go out and** see her riches, **and** partake in her **rejoicing with heaven** and earth. I should **not then** be a persuader **to them of** studying much then, after two or three **years that they have** well laid their grounds, **but to** ride **out in companies with** prudent and staid guides to all **the quarters of the land."**

The whole treatise is full of wisdom, and deserves to be studied again and again. Visionary as it may appear to some at first sight, if translated into the language of our own day, it will be found to abound with sound, practical advice. "Only," Milton says in conclusion, "I believe that this is not a bow for every man to shoot who counts himself a teacher, but will require sinews almost equal to those which Homer gave Ulysses; yet I am persuaded that it may prove much more easy in the essay than it now seems at a distance, and much more illustrious if God have so decided and this age have spirit and capacity enough to apprehend."

Almost while Milton was writing this treatise, he might have seen an attempt to realize something of his ideal in Port Royal. What a charm does this name awaken! Yet how few of us have made a pilgrimage to that secluded valley! Here we find for the first time in the modern world the highest gifts of the greatest men of a country applied to the business of education. Arnauld, Lancelot, Nicole did not commence by being educational philosophers. They began with a small school, and developed their method as they proceeded. Their success has seldom been surpassed.

But a more lasting memorial than their pupils are the books which they sent out, which bear the name of their cloister. The *Port Royal Logic*, *General Grammar*, *Greek*, *Latin*, *Italian*, and *Spanish Grammars*, the *Garden of Greek Roots* which taught Greek to Gibbon, the *Port Royal Geometry*, and their translations of the classics held the first place among school books for more than a century.

The success of the Jansenists was too much for the jealousy of the Jesuits. Neither piety, nor wit, nor virtue could save them. A light was quenched which would have given an entirely different direction to the education of France and of Europe. No one can visit without emotion that retired nook which lies hidden among the forests of Versailles, where the old brick dove-cot, the pillars of the church, the trees of the desert alone remain to speak to us of Pascal, Racine, and the Mére Angelique.

The principles of Port Royal found some supporters in a later time, in the better days of French education before monarchism and militarism had crushed the life out of the nation. Rollin is never mentioned without the epithet *bon*, a testimony to his wisdom, virtue and simplicity. Fenelon may be reckoned as belonging to the same school, but he was more fitted to mix and grapple with mankind.

CHARLES ROLLIN, 1661-1741

ABP. FENELON, 1651-1715

No history of education would be complete without the name of August Hermann Francke, the founder of the school of Pietists, and of a number of institutions which now form almost a suburb in the town of Halle to which his labors were devoted. The first scenes of his activity were Leipzig and Dresden; but in 1692, at the age of 29, he was made pastor of Glaucha, near Halle, and professor in the newly established university.

AUGUST HERMANN FRANCKE,
1663-1727

Three years later he commenced his poor school with a capital of seven guelders which he found in the poor box of his house. At his death in 1727 he left behind him the following institutions:—a pædagogium, or training college, with eighty-two scholars and seventy teachers receiving education, and attendants; the Latin school of the orphan asylum, with three inspectors, thirty-two teachers, four hundred scholars, and ten servants; the German town schools, with four inspectors, ninety-eight teachers, eight female teachers, and one thousand seven hundred and twenty-five boys and girls. The establishment for orphan children contained one hundred boys, thirty-four girls, and ten attendants. A cheap public dining-table was attended by two hundred and fifty-five students and three hundred and sixty poor scholars, and besides this there was an apothecary's and a bookseller's shop.

Francke's principles of education were strictly religious. Hebrew was included in his curriculum, but the heathen classics were treated with slight respect. The *Homilies* of Macarius were read in the place of Thucydides. As might be expected, the rules laid down for discipline and moral training breathed a spirit of deep affection and sympathy.

Francke's great merit, however, is to have left us a model of institutions by which children of all ranks may receive an education to fit them for any position in life. The Franckesche Stiftungen are still, next to the university, the centre of the intellectual life of Halle, and the different schools which they contain give instruction to 3,500 children.

We now come to the book which has had more influence than any other on the education of later times. The *Emile* of Rousseau was published in 1762. It produced an astounding effect throughout Europe. Those were days when the whole cultivated world vibrated to any touch of new philosophy. French had superseded Latin as the general medium of thought. French learning stood in the same relation to the rest of Europe as German learning does now: and any discovery of D'Alembert, Rousseau, or Maupertuis travelled with inconceivable speed from Versailles to Schonbrunn, from the Spree to the Neva. Kant in his distant home of Königsberg broke for one day through his habits, more regular than the town clock, and staid at home to study the new revelation.

JEAN JACQUES ROUSSEAU,
1712-1778

The burthen of Rousseau's message was nature, such a nature as never did and never will exist, but still a name for an ideal worthy of our struggles. He revolted against the false civilization which he saw around him; he was penetrated with sorrow at the shams of government and society, at the misery of the poor existing side by side with the heartlessness of the rich. The child should be the pupil of nature.

He lays great stress on the earliest education. The first year of life is in every respect the most important. Nature must be closely followed. The child's tears are petitions which should be granted. The naughtiness of children comes from weakness; make the child strong and he will be good. Children's destructiveness is a form of activity. Do not be too anxious to make children talk; be satisfied with a small vocabulary. Lay aside all padded caps and baby jumpers. Let children learn to walk by learning that it hurts them to fall. Do not insist so much on the duty of obedience as on the necessity of submission to natural laws. Do not argue too much with children; educate the heart to wish for right actions; before all things study nature. The chief moral principle is *do no one harm*.

Emile is to be taught by the real things of life, by observation and experience. At twelve years old he is scarcely to know what a book is; to be able to read and write at fifteen is quite enough. We must first make him a man, and that chiefly by athletic exercises. Educate his sight to measure, count, and weight accurately; teach him to draw; tune his ear to time and harmony: give him simple food, but let him eat as much as he likes. Thus at twelve years old Emile is a real child of nature. His carriage and bearing are fair and confident, his nature open and candid, his speech simple and to the point; his ideas are few but clear; he knows nothing by learning, much by experience. He has read deeply in the book of nature. His mind is not on his tongue but in his head. He speaks only one language, but knows what he is saying, and can do what he cannot describe. Routine and custom are unknown to him; authority and example affect him not: he does what he thinks right. He understands nothing of duty and obedience, but he will do what you ask him, and will expect a similar service of you in return. His strength and body are fully developed; he is first-rate at running, jumping, and judging distances. Should he die at this age he will so far have lived his life.

From twelve to fifteen Emile's practical education is to continue. He is still to avoid books which teach not learning itself but to appear learned. He is to be taught and to practise some handicraft. Half the value of education is to waste time wisely, to tide over dangerous years with safety, until the character is better able to stand temptation.

At fifteen a new epoch commences. The passions are awakened; the care of the teacher should now redouble; he should never leave the helm. Emile having gradually acquired the love of himself and of those immediately about him, will begin to love his kind. Now is the time to teach him history, and the machinery of society, the world as it is and as it might be. Still an encumbrance of useless and burdensome knowledge is to be avoided. Between this age and manhood Emile learns all that it is necessary for him to know.

It is, perhaps, strange that a book in many respects so wild and fantastic should have produced so great a practical effect. In pursuance of its precepts, children went about naked, were not allowed to read, and when they grew up wore the simplest clothes, and cared for little learning except the study of nature and Plutarch.

The catastrophe of the French Revolution has made the importance of Emile less apparent to us. Much of the heroism of that time is doubtless due to the exaltation produced by the sweeping away of abuses, and the approach of a brighter age. But we must not forget that the first generation of Emile was just thirty years old in 1792; that many of the Girondins, the Marseillais, the soldiers and generals of Carnot and Napoleon had been bred in that hardy school. There is no more interesting chapter in the history of education than the tracing back of epochs of special activity to the obscure source from which they arose. Thus the Whigs of the Reform Bill sprang from the wits of Edinburgh, the heroes of the Rebellion from the divines who translated the Bible, the martyrs of the Revolution from the philosophers of the Encyclopædia.

BASEDOW 53

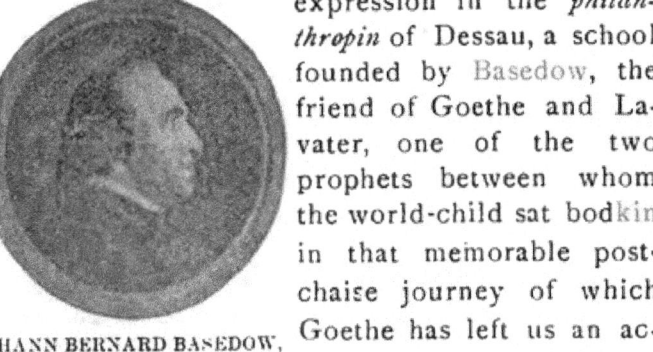

JOHANN BERNARD BASEDOW,
1723-1790

The teaching of Rousseau found its practical expression in the *philanthropin* of Dessau, a school founded by Basedow, the friend of Goethe and Lavater, one of the two prophets between whom the world-child sat bodkin in that memorable post-chaise journey of which Goethe has left us an account. The principles of the teaching given in this establishment were very much those of Comenius, the combination of words and things.

An amusing account of the instruction given in this school, which at this time consisted of only thirteen pupils, has come down to us, a translation of which is given in the excellent work of Mr. Quick on educational reformers*. The little ones have gone through the oddest performances. They play at "word of command". Eight or ten stand in line like soldiers, and Herr Wolke is officer. He gives the word in Latin, and they must do whatever he says. For instance when he says "*Claudite oculos*", they all shut their eyes; when he says "*Circumspicite*", they look about them; "*Imitamini sutorem*", they draw their waxed thread like cobblers. Herr Wolke gives a thousand different commands in the drollest fashion.

Another game, "the hiding game", may also be described. Some one writes a name and hides it

---

Pp. 193-197 of the Reading Circle edition, Syracuse, N. Y.

from the children, the name of some part of the body, or of a plant or animal, or metal, and the children guess what it is. Whoever guesses right gets an apple or a piece of cake; one of the visitors wrote "*intestina*", and told the children it was part of the body. Then the guessing began; one guessed *caput*, another *nasus*, another *os*, another *manus, pes, digiti, pectus*, and so forth for a long time, but one of them hits it at last.

Next Herr Wolke wrote the name of a beast or quadruped, then came the guesses, *leo, ursus, camelus, elephas*, and so on, till one guessed right it was *mus*. Then a town was written, and they guessed Lisbon, Madrid, Paris, London, till a child won with St. Petersburg.

They had another game which was this. Herr Wolke gave the command in Latin, and they imitated the noises of different animals, and made the visitors laugh till they were tired. They roared like lions, crowed like cocks, mewed like cats, just as they were bid.

Yet Kant found a great deal to praise in this school, and spoke of its influence as one of the best hopes of the future, and as "the only school where the teachers had liberty to act according to their own methods and schemes, and where they were in free communication both among themselves and with all learned men throughout Germany."

IMMANUEL KANT, 1724-1804

A more successful laborer in the same school was Salzmann, who bought the property of Schnepfenthal, near Gotha, in 1784, and established a school there, which still exists as a flourishing institution. He gave full scope to the doctrines of the philanthropists; the limits of learning were enlarged; study became a pleasure instead of a pain; scope was given for healthy exercise; the school became light, airy, and cheerful. A charge of superficiality and weakness was brought against this method of instruction; but the gratitude which our generation of teachers owes to the unbounded love and faith of these devoted men cannot be denied or refused.

The end of the 18th century saw a great development given to classical studies. The names of Cellarius, Gesner, Ernesti, and Heyne are perhaps more celebrated as scholars than as schoolmasters. To them we owe the great importance attached to the study of the classics, both on the Continent and in England. They brought into the schools the philology which F. A. Wolfe had organized for the universities.

Pestalozzi, on the other hand, was completely and entirely devoted to education. His greatest merit is that he set an example of absolute self-abnegation; that he lived with his pupils, played, starved, and suffered with them; and clung to their minds and hearts with an affectionate sympathy which revealed to him every minute difference of character and disposition.

Pestalozzi was born at Zurich in 1746. His father

JOHANN HEINRICH PESTALOZZI, 1746-1827

Rüdenplatz, Zurich. The middle house was Pestalozzi's birthplace.

died when he was young, and he was brought up by his mother. His earliest years were spent in schemes for improving the condition of the people. The death of his friend Bluntschli turned him from political schemes, and induced him to devote himself to education. He married at 23, and bought a piece of waste land in Aargau, where he attempted the cultivation of madder. Pestalozzi knew nothing of business, and the plan failed. Before this he had opened his farm-house as a school; but in 1780 he had to give this up also.

His first book published at this time was *The Evening Hours of a Hermit*, a series of aphorisms and reflections. This was followed by his masterpiece, *Leonard and Gertrude*, an account of the gradual reformation, first of a household, and then of a whole village, by the efforts of a good and devoted woman. It was read with avidity in Germany, and the name of Pestalozzi was rescued from obscurity. His attempts to follow up his first literary success were failures.

The French invasion of Switzerland in 1798 brought into relief his truly heroic character. A number of children were left in Canton Unterwalden on the shores of the Lake of Luzerne without parents, home,

STANZ

food, or shelter. Pestalozzi collected a number of them into a deserted convent, and spent his energies in reclaiming them.

"I was," he says, "from morning till evening, almost alone in their midst. Everything which was

done for their body or soul proceeded from my hand. Every assistance, every help in time of need, every teaching which they received came immediatly from me. My hand lay in their hand, my eye rested on their eye, my tears flowed with theirs, and my laughter accompanied theirs. They were out of the world, they were out of Stanz; they were with me, and I was with them. Their soup was mine; their drink was mine. I had nothing; I had no housekeeper, no friend, no servants around me; I had them alone. Were they well I stood in their midst; were they ill, I was at their side. I slept in the middle of them. I was the last who went to bed at night, the first who rose in the morning. Even in bed I prayed and taught with them until they were asleep,—they wished it to be so." Thus he passed the winter; but in June, 1799, the building was required by the French for a hospital, and the children were dispersed.

We have dwelt especially on this episode of Pestalozzi's life, because in this devotion lay his strength. In 1801 he gave an exposition of his ideas on education in the book *How Gertrude teaches her Children**. His method is to proceed from the easier to the more difficult—to begin with observation, to pass from observation to consciousness, from consciousness to speech. Then come measuring, drawing, writing, numbers, and so reckoning.

---

* How Gertrude teaches her Children. An attempt to help mothers to teach their own children, and an account of the method. A report to the Society of the Friends of Education, Burgdorf, by Johann Heinrich Pestalozzi. Translated by Lucy E. Holland and Frances E. Turner, and edited, with introduction and notes, by Ebenezer Cooke. 12:308. $1.50. Syracuse, N. Y., C. W. Bardeen, 1894.

In 1799 he had been enabled to establish a school

BURGDORF

at Burgdorf, where he remained till 1804. In 1802, he went as deputy to Paris, and did his best to interest Napoleon in a scheme of national education; but the great conqueror said that he could not trouble himself about the alphabet.

In 1805 he removed to Yverdun on the Lake of Neufchatel, and for twenty years worked steadily at his task. He was visited by all who took interest in education—Talleyrand, Capo d'Istria, and Madame de Stael. He was praised by Wilhelm von Humboldt and by Fichte. His pupils included Ramsauer, Delbruck, Blochmann, Carl Ritter, Froebel, and Zeller.

YVERDUN

About 1815 dissensensions broke out among the teachers of the school, and Pestalozzi's last ten years were chequered by weariness and sorrow. In 1825 he retired to Neuhof, the home of his youth; and after writing the adventures of his life, and his last work, the *Swan's Song*, he died in 1827.

JOHANN GOTTLIEB FICHTE
1762-1814

As he said himself, the real work of his life did not lie in Burgdorf or in Yverdun, the products rather

The castle at Yverdun where Pestalozzi established in 1805 his training school. It is the building on

of his weakness than of his strength. It lay in the principles of education which he practised, the development of his observation, the training of the whole man, the sympathetic application of the teacher to the taught, of which he left an example in his six months' labors at Stanz. He showed what truth there was in the principles of Comenius and Rousseau, in the union of training with information, and the submissive following of nature; he has had the

The Schoolhouse at Birr, with Pestalozzi's Memorial

deepest effect on all branches of education since his time, and his influence is far from being exhausted.

Statue in Pestalozzi Square, Yverdun. Inscription: "To Pestalozzi, 1746-1827. This monument was erected by popular subscription in 1890."

The *Emile* of Rousseau was the point of departure for an awakened interest in educational theories which has continued unto the present day. Few thinkers of eminence during the last hundred years have failed to offer their contributions more or less directly on this subject. Poets like Richter, Herder and Goethe, philosophers such as Kant, Fichte, Hegel, Schleiermacher and Schopenhauer, psychologists such as Herbart and Beneke, have left directions for our guidance.

ARTHUR SCHOPENHAUER,
1788-1860

Indeed, during this time the science of education, or pædagogics, as the Germans call it, may have been said to have come into existence. It has attracted but little attention in England; but it is an important subject of study at all German universities, and we may hope that the example given by the establishment of chairs of education in the Scotch universities may soon be followed by the other great centres of instruction in Great Britain.

JOHANN FRIEDRICH HERBART
1776-1841

Jean Paul called his book *Levana* after the Roman

JOHANN PAUL FRIEDRICH
RICHTER, 1763-1825

goddess to whom the father dedicated his new-born child, in token that he intended to rear it to manhood. He lays great stress on the preservation of individuality of character, a merit which he possessed himself in so high a degree.

The second part of *Wilhelm Meister* is in the main a treatise upon education. The essays of Carlyle have made us familiar with the mysteries of the pædagogic province, the solemn gestures of the three reverences, the long cloisters which contain the history of God's dealings with the human race. The most characteristic passage is that which de-

JOHANN WOLFGANG von GOETHE
1749-1832

scribes the father's return to the country of education after a year's absence. As he is riding alone, wondering in what guise he will meet his son, a multitude of horses rush by at full gallop. "The monstrous hurly-b u r l y whirls past the wanderer; a fair boy among the keepers looks at him in surprise, pulls in, leaps down, and embraces his father."

He then learns that an agricultural life had not suited his son, that the superiors had discovered that he was fond of animals, and had set him to that occupation for which nature had destined him.

The system of Jacotot has aroused great interest in this country. Its author was born at Dijon in 1770. In 1815 he retired to Louvain and became professor there, and director of the Belgian military school. He died in 1840. His method of teaching is based on three principles:

JOSEPH JACOTOT, 1770-1840

1. All men have an equal intelligence.

2. Every man has received from God the faculty of being able to instruct himself.

3. Every thing is in every thing.

The first of these principles is certainly wrong, although Jacotot tried to explain it by asserting that, although men had the same intelligence, they differed widely in the will to make use of it. Still it is important to assert that nearly all men are capable of receiving some intellectual education, provided the studies to which they are directed are wide enough to engage their faculties, and the means taken to interest them are sufficiently ingenious. The second principle lays down that it is more necessary to stimulate the pupil to learn for himself, than to teach him didactically.

The third principle explains the process which Jacotot adopted. To one learning a language for the first time he would give a short passage of a few lines, and encourage the pupil to study first the words, then the letters, then the grammar, then the full meaning of the expressions, until by iteration and accretion a single paragraph took the place of an entire literature. Much may be effected by this method in the hands of a skilful teacher, but a charlatan might make it an excuse for ignorance and neglect.

Among those who have improved the methods of teaching, we must mention Bell and Lancaster, the joint discoverers of the method of mutual instruction, which, if it has not effected everything which its founders expected of it, has produced the system of pupil-teachers which is common in our schools. Froebel also deserves an honorable place as the founder of the Kindergarten, a means of teaching young children by playing and amusement. His plans, which have a far wider significance than this limited development of them, are likely to be fruitful of results to future workers.

ANDREW BELL, 1753-1832

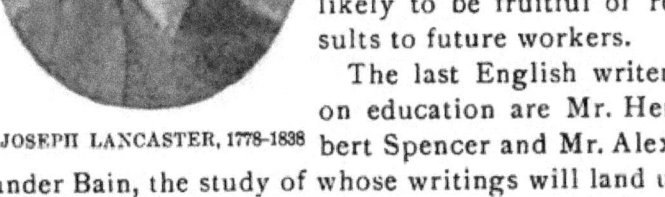

JOSEPH LANCASTER, 1778-1838

The last English writers on education are Mr. Herbert Spencer and Mr. Alexander Bain, the study of whose writings will land us in those regions of pedagogics which have been most recently explored.

We need not follow Mr. Spencer into his defence of science as the worthiest object of study, or in his rules for moral and physical training, except to say they are sound and practical. In writing of intellectual education, he insists that we shall attain the best results by closely studying the development of the mind, and availing ourselves of the whole amount of force which nature puts at our disposal. The mind of every being is naturally active and vigorous, indeed it is never at rest. But for its healthy growth it must have something to work upon, and, therefore, the teacher must watch its movements with the most sympathetic care, in order to supply exactly that food which it requires at any particular time. In this way a much larger cycle of attainments can be compassed than by the adoption of any programme or curriculum, however carefully drawn up.

HERBERT SPENCER, 1820—

It is no good to teach what is not remembered; the strength of memory depends on attention, and attention depends upon interest. To teach without interest is to work like Sisyphus and the Danaides. Arouse interest if you can, rather by high means than by low means. But it is a saving of power to make use of interest which you have already existing, and which, unless dried up or distorted by injudicious violence, will naturally lead the mind into all the knowledge which it is capable of receiving.

Therefore, never from the first force a child's attention; leave off a study the moment it becomes wearisome, never let a child do what it does not like, only take care that when its liking is in activity a choice of good as well as evil shall be given to it.

Mr. Bain's writings on education, which are contained in some articles in the *Fortnightly Review*, and in two articles in *Mind* (Nos. v. and vii.) are extremely valuable. Perhaps the most interesting part of them consists in his showing how what may be called the "correlation of forces in man" helps us to a right education. From this we learn that emotion may be transformed into intellect, that sensation may exhaust the brain as much as thought, and we may infer that the chief duty of the schoolmaster is to stimulate the powers of each brain under his charge to the fullest activity, and to apportion them in that ratio which will best conduce to the most complete and harmonious development of the individual.

It seems to follow from this sketch of the history of education that, in spite of the great advances which have been made of late years, the science of education is still far in advance of the art. Schoolmasters are still spending their best energies in teaching subjects which have been universally condemned by educational reformers for the last two hundred years. The education of every public school is a farrago of rules, principles, and customs derived from every age of teaching, from the most modern to the most remote. It is plain that the science and art of teaching will never be established on a firm basis until it is organized on the model of the sister art of medicine. We must pursue the patient methods of induction by which other sciences have reached the stature of maturity; we must discover some means of registering and tabulating results; we must invent a phraseology and nomenclature which will enable results to be accurately recorded; we must place education in its proper position among the sciences of observation. A philosopher who should succeed in doing this would be venerated by future ages as the creator of the art of teaching.

It only remains now to give some account of the very large literature of the subject.

The history of education was not investigated till the beginning of the present century, and since then little original research has been made except by Germans. Whilst acknowledging our great obligations to the German historians, we cannot but regret that all the investigations have belonged to the same nation. For instance, one of the best treatises on education written in the 16th century is Mulcaster's *Positions*, which has never been reprinted, and is now a literary curiosity.

Mangelsdorf and Ruhkopf attempted histories of education at the end of the last century, but the first work of note was F. H. Ch. Schwarz's *Geschichte d. Erziehung* (1813). A. H. Niemeyer, a very influential writer, was one of the first to insist on the importance of making use of all that has been handed down to us, and with this practical object in view he has given us an *Ueberblick der allgemeinen Geschichte der Erziehung*.

AUGUST HERMANN NIEMEYER,
1754-1828

Other writers followed; but from the time of its appearance till within the last few years, by far the most readable and the most read work on the history of education was that of Karl von Raumer. Raumer, however, is too chatty and too religious to pass for "*wissenschaftlich*", and the standard history is now that of Karl Schmidt. The Roman Catholics have not been content to adopt the works of Protestants, but have histories of their own. These are the very pleasing sketches of L. Kellner and the somewhat larger history by Stoeckl.

KARL GEORG von RAUMER
1783-1865

When we come to writers who have produced sketches or shorter histories, we find the list in Germany a very long one. Among the best books of this kind are Fried. Dittes's *Geschichte* and Dröse's *Pädagogische Characterbilder*. An account of this literature will be found in J. Chr. G. Schurmann's paper among the *Pädagogische Studien*, edited by Dr. Reiss.

For biographies the pædagogic cyclopædias may be consulted, of which the first is the *Encyclopadie des gesammten Erziehungswesens* of K. A. Schmid, a great work in 11 or 12 vols. not yet completed, although the second edition of the early vols. is already announced. The Roman Catholics have also begun a large encyclopædia edited by Rolfus and Pfister. No similar work has been published in France, but a *Cyclopædia of Education* in one volume has lately been issued in New York (Steiger,—the editors are Kiddle and Schem), and in this there are articles by English as well as American writers*. In French the *Esquisse d'un systeme complet d' Education*, by Th. Fritz (Strasburg, 1841), has a sketch of the history, which as a sketch is worth notice. Jules Paroz has written a useful little *Histoire* which would have been more valuable if it had been longer.

In English, though we have no investigators of the history of education, we have a fairly large literature on the subject, but it belongs almost exclusively to the United States. The great work of Henry Barnard, the *American Journal of Education*, in 25 vols., has valuable papers on almost every part of our subject, many of them translated from the German, but there are also original papers on our old English educational writers and extracts from their works. This is by far the most valuable work in our language on the history of education.

HENRY BARNARD, 1811—

---

* A more recent publication is "Sonnenschein's Cyclopaedia of Education: a handbook on all subjects connected with education (its history, theory, and practice) comprising articles by eminent educational specialists. The whole arranged and edited by Alfred Ewen Fletcher." 8:560, $3.75. Syracuse, N. Y., C. W. Bardeen, 1889.

The small volumes published in America with the title of "History of Education" do not deserve notice. In England may be mentioned the article on education by Mr. James Mill, published in the early editions of the *Encyclopædia Britannica*, and R. H. Quick's most excellent *Essays on Educational Reformers*, published in 1868*. Since then Mr. Leitch of Glasgow has issued a volume called *Practical Educationists*, which deals with English and Scotch reformers, as well as with Comenius and Pestalozzi. Now that professorships of education have been established we may hope for some original research. The first professor appointed was the late Joseph Payne, a name well-known to those among us who have studied the theory of education. The professorship was started by the College of Preceptors. At Edinburgh and at St. Andrews professors have since been elected by the Bell Trustees.

ROBERT HEBERT QUICK,
1831-1891

Valuable reports as to the state of education in the various countries that possess a national system were presented to the English schools Inquiry Commission in 1867 and 1868, by inspectors specially

---

*Essays on Educational Reformers by Robert Hebert Quick. Reading Circle Edition, with Notes and Illustrations. 16:420. $1.00. Syracuse, N. Y., 1896. C. W. Bardeen.

appointed to investigate the subject. The reports on the Common School System of the United States and Canada, by the Rev. James Fraser, on the Burgh Schools in Scotland by D. R. Fearon, and on Secondary Education in France, Germany, Switzerland and Italy, by Matthew Arnold, are included in Parliamentary Papers [3857], 1867, and [3966 v.], 1868. (O. B.)

MATTHEW ARNOLD, 1822-1895

NOTES AND REFERENCES

GENERAL SOURCES OF INFORMATION

Schmidt and Raumer are the great authorities on the history of education. Copious translations from Raumer are contained in Barnard's *American Journal of Education*, and the portions relating to German education are collected in Barnard's *German Teachers and Educators*.

Paroz's *Histoire Universelle* is elegantly written, and contains, within a moderate compass, an admirable summary of educational history.

For the study of special topics, Mr. Quick's *Educational Reformers* cannot be too highly recommended. Mr. Leitch writes with much less critical discernment, and some of his subjects are of minor importance, but his work may be read with great profit.

As a critical history of educational doctrines, the work of Compayré is of incomparable value. Though he is occupied chiefly with French pedagogy, he discusses almost every aspect of the educational problem, and always with great penetration and clearness.

Williams's *History of Modern Education* is the most recent work, and particularly adapted to American schools.

The Reform in Education

The Reformation marks the further limit of the modern period of educational history; and these beginnings of educational reform deserve very careful study. The compilation of Souquet, and particularly his introduction, will be found very helpful. Schmidt, Raumer, Compayré, and Paroz will supply an abundance of material bearing on this topic. For a study of the recognized educational reformers, the works of Mr. Quick and Mr. Barnard are invaluable.

Rousseau and his Émile

With the progress of educational science, the influence of Rousseau is perceptibly and steadily growing, and a careful study of the Émile is becoming imperative. This study may now be conveniently prosecuted at first hand through the compilation just made by Souquet. The fairest estimate of Rousseau that I have yet seen, is contained in the second volume of Compayré.

Joseph Payne

By far the most valuable of recent contributions to educational literature from English sources, is Joseph Payne's *Lectures*, edited by his son, and containing an introduction by Mr. Quick. Mr. Payne was a disciple of Jacotot, and in this volume he gives an admirable exposition of his master's system. Outside of England, the doctrines of Jacotot enjoy but little consideration; but there are very few modern writers on education who are more worthy of serious study. Each of his paradoxes embodies a doctrine worth the knowing.

The Old Education and the New

In studying the later developments of educational thought, it is essential to keep in mind the fact that they embody a reaction against antagonistic doctrines; and the further fact that "the suppression of an error is commonly followed by the temporary ascendancy of a contrary one". There are sharp points of contrast between the old education and the new. Each has a measure of truth and a measure of error; each is right in what it admits and wrong in what it denies; and so each is in a great degree the complement of the other. The truth will be found to lie somewhere between the two extremes.

Pestalozzi

No just and adequate estimate of Pestalozzi's influence can be formed unless his doctrines are contrasted with those that he sought to supplant. We are living in the midst of transformations that have been wrought through the influence of Pestalozzianism; and so the present does not furnish the criteria by which to estimate the importance of this innovation in educational thought.

Every new Phase in Education embodies an Idea.

No new movement in education can be adequately interpreted without taking into account the cognate phases of thought, social, political, philosophical, and religious, with which it co-existed. Some dominant idea will be found to underlie every system of educational doctrine. When the principle of AUTHORITY was dominant in church and state, it was also dominant in the schools, and prescribed its methods of discipline and of instruction; and the decline of authority in church and state has induced a corresponding change in the methods of the school. The philosophical idea that is dominant in the new education is that of DEVELOPMENT; and in this country when the professional teacher must count with his constituents, there is the concurrent and modifying idea of UTILITY.

NEED OF A GENERAL HISTORY OF EDUCATIONAL DOCTRINES

The construction of a general history of education, for the express purpose of tracing the rise and progress of all the marked phases of educational thought, and characterized by the critical discernment that gives such charm and value to the work of Compayré, is a thing greatly to be desired at this time when questions of school policy are beginning to be discussed on a scientific basis.

BUISSON's *Dictionnaire de la Pédagogie*

Buisson's *Dictionnare de la Pédagogie* is on all accounts the most valuable book of reference that can be commended to the professional teacher. Scarcely any other book will be required to supplement this SHORT HISTORY OF EDUCATION, so complete is its treatment of historical and biographical subjects.

In English, the latest general compilation is Sonnenschein's *Cyclopaedia of Education*, the American edition of which is published by C. W. Bardeen, Syracuse, N. Y.

COMENIUS

COMENIUS

COMPARATIVE TABLE OF DATES

Erasmus..........1467–1536	Rousseau..........1712–1778
Luther............1483–1546	Diderot...........1713–1784
Sturm............1507–1589	Condillac.........1715–1780
Ascham..........1515–1568	Basedow..........1723–**1790**
Ramus...........1515–1572	Kant.............**1724–1804**
Montaigne........1533–1592	Pestalozzi........**1746–1827**
Bacon............1561–1626	Jacotot...........1770–1840
Ratke............1571–1635	Fellenberg........1771–1844
Comenius 1592–1671	Froebel 1782–1852
Descartes........1596–1650	Diesterweg........1790–1866
Milton...........1608–1674	Cousin...........1792–1867
Locke............1632–1704	Beneke...........1798–1856
Francke..........1663–1727	Spencer..........1820 —

OUTLINE BIOGRAPHY

1592. Born at Nivnitz, a village of Moravia, on the confines of Hungary; early an orphan; began his education at the age of 16.

1610. Went to the Universities of Herborn and Heidelberg; then travelled for ten years in Holland and perhaps in England.

1614. Returned to Bohemia and became director of the school in Prerau, where he published his first work, *Grammaticae Facilioris Praecepta*.

1618. Became pastor of the Bohemian Brethren in Fulneck.

1621. By the sack of Fulneck, lost his property, books, and MS.; and for several years was a refugee from religious persecution.

1627. By the Edict of July 31, followed the Moravians into permanent banishment and took refuge in Lissa Poland, where he wrote his *Janua Linguarum Reserata*.

1641. Went to London by the invitation of Parliament, at the instance of Samuel Hartlib (the friend of Milton), who, in 1631, had published at Oxford a part of the *Didactica Magna*.

1642. Went on an educational mission into Sweden, and thence to Elbing, Prussia.

1648. Made Bishop of the Moravians and took up his residence again in Lissa.

1650. Went to Patak, Hungary, to establish a model school on the principles of his *Pansophia*. While in Patak he wrote the most popular of his works, the *Orbis Sensualium Pictus*. On leaving Patak he returned to Lissa.

1656. On the burning of Lissa by the Polish Catholics, took refuge in Amsterdam.

1671. November 15, died at Amsterdam.

APPRECIATION

"The system which he sketched will be found to foreshadow the education of the future."

"He was one of the first advocates of the teaching of science in schools."

"His kindness, gentleness, and sympathy, make him the forerunner of Pestalozzi."—*Encycl. Brit.*

"Comenius founded nothing durable and distinctive; he was but an admirable precursor. His work had to be again taken up, continued and perfected, by the educators of the following century, the most of whom did not know him—so soon was he forgotten—and who followed in his foot-steps, like Rousseau and Pestalozzi, without suspecting it."—*Buisson.*

"A Protestant grammarian and theologian; was a mad-man, but from this mad man we have a book entitled *Janua Linguarum Reserata*, which was translated not only into twelve European languages, but also into the principal languages of Asia "—*Enc. Méthodique.*

"Of boundless generosity and intelligence, he embraced all knowledge and every nationality. Through every country—Poland, Hungary, Sweden, England, Holland—he went teaching, first Peace, and then the means of peace—Universal Fraternity. He wrote a hundred works, taught in a hundred cities. Sooner or later, the scattered members of this great man, that he left upon every route, will be reunited."—*Michelet.*

"As a school reformer he was the forerunner of Rousseau, Basedow, and Pestalozzi, suggested a mode of instruction which renders learning attractive to children by pictures and illustrations, and wrote the first pictorial school-book."—*New Amer. Cycl.*

"Comenius is a grand and venerable figure of sorrow. Wandering, persecuted, and homeless, during the terrible and desolating thirty years' war, he never despaired; but with enduring and faithful truth, labored unweariedly to prepare youth, by a better education, for a better future. His undespairing aspirations seem to have lifted up, in a large part of Europe, many good men, prostrated by the terrors of the times, and to have inspired them with the hope that by a pious and wise system of education, there would be reared up a race of men more pleasing to God."—*Raumer.*

BIBLIOGRAPHY

I

SOURCES OF INFORMATION

1. Cyclopædia of Education. **C. W.** Bardeen, Syracuse, 1889.

2. Buisson's Dictionnaire de Pédagogie et d'Instruction Primaire. 1re Partie. Paris, 1887.

3. Quick's Essays on Educational Reformers, Chapter VII. Syracuse, 1896.

4. **Histoire** Critique des Doctrines de L'Éducation en France. Par G. Compayré. Paris, 1879. Tome Premier, pp. 256-263.

5. Michelet. **Nos Fils.** Paris, 1877.

6. Jules Paroz. **Histoire** Universelle de la Pédagogie. Paris, pp. 203-216.

7. Karl Schmidt, Geschichte der Pädagogik. Cöthen. 1873-1876. pp. 366-398, Dritter Band.

8. Karl von Raumer, Geschichte der Pädagogik, Stuttgart. 1857. pp. 48-100, Zweiter Theil.

9. Barnard's American **Journal of** Education. Vol. V., pp. 257-298. [A translation of No. 8.] Also Vol. VI, p. 585. [On the *Orbis Pictus*.]

10. Bayle's **Historical and Critical** Dictionary. London, 1735.

11. Carpzov. Religionsuntersuchung der Böhmischen und Mährischen Brüder.

12. Gindely. Ueber des J. A. Comenius' Leben und Wirksamkeit in der Fremde. (In the proceedings of the Vienna Academy of Science. Vienna, 1855.)

13. Leutbecher. Johann Amos Comenius, Lehrkunst. Leipzig, 1853.

14. Dr. Eugen Pappenheim. Amos Comenius, der Begründer der neuen Pädagogik. Berlin, 1871.

15. K. A. Schmid. Pädagogisches Handbuch fur Schule und Haus. Gotha, 1877.

16. Seyffarth, L. W. J. A. Comenius, nach seinem Leben und seiner pädagogischen Bedeutung. Leipzig, 1871.

17. Beiträge zur Pädagogik. Ueber die historische Darstellung der pädagogischen Jdeen mit besonderer Beziehung auf Rousseau und Comenius. Löwenberg, 1875.

18. Comenius, Amos, Die Mutterschule. Aufs Neue hrsg. v. Herm. Schröter. Weissenfels, 1864.

19. Hoffmeister, Herm. Comenius und Pestalozzi als Begründer der Volksschule, wissenschaftlich dargestellt, 8vo. Berlin, 1877.

20. Laurie, S. S John Amos Gomenius, his Life and Work, 16mo. Syracuse, 1892.

21. Butler, Nicholas Murray. The Place of Comenius in the History of Education, 16mo. Syracuse, 1892.

22. Maxwell, W. H. The Text-Books of Comenius, 8vo. Syracuse, 1892.

NOTE.—"We are assured that **France** will soon have two works upon Comenius, which, **we** hope, will be only a prelude to important studies relating to this eminent educator; one by M. Rieder and the other by M. Diog. Bertrand."—*Dic. de Pédag.*

II

WORKS

1. Didactica Opera Omnia ab anno **1627** ad 1657 continuata. Amstelodamus, Chr. Conradus et Gabr. **a Roy,** 1657. 4 part. in-fol., avec port., 482, 462, 1064 et 110 col.—*Brunet.*

This edition **contains** the collected works **of Comenius, edited by** himself, and published by the **munificence of his Patron,** Lorenzo de **Geer.**

2. **Comenius, Johann Amos.** Ausgewählte Schriften, **Mutterschule, Pansophia,** Pangnosie, etc. Uebersetzt und mit **Erläute**rungen versehen von Ju. **Beeger** und Johann Leutbecher, **8vo.** Leipzig.

3. **Comenius's** (John Amos) Visible World; or a Nomenclature and Pictures, of all the chief things that are in the World, etc., illustrated with **150 curious rude** woodcuts, 12mo. 1777.

4. The Orbis Pictus of John Amos Comenius, 8vo. Syracuse, 1887.

5. **Karl** Richter. Pädagogische Bibliothek. Eine Sammlung der wichtigsten pädagogischen Schriften alter und neuerer Zeit. Leipzig.

Volume third contains the *Didactica Magna,* an

appreciation of it, a Life of Comenius, and notes. Edited by Julius Beeger and Franz Zoubek.

6. Dr. Th. Lion. Bibliothek pädagogischer Classiker. Langensalza, 1875.—Contains German translations of the pedagogical works of Comenius.

7. Johann Amos Comenius. Grosse Unterichtslehre (*Didactica Magna*), mit einer Einleitung von Gustav Adolf Linder. Wien, 1877.

The Three Great Pedagogical Works of Comenius

Comenius was a very prolific writer, being the author of more than eighty publications, written in Slavic (Czechic), Latin, and German; but he owes his fame to the three following works.

I. DIDACTICA MAGNA, SEU OMNES OMNIA DOCENDI ARTIFICIUM.

This great work was begun in 1627, while Comenius was living in exile at Sloupna. It was finished in 1632, but remained in manuscript till 1849, when it was published in the original language (Czechic).

A translation of a part of the *Didactica Magna*, under the title of *Prodromus Pansophiae*, was published in London in 1639, through the mediation of Samuel Hartlib, by whose influence Parliament invited Comenius to England to organize a reform in public education. Buisson, in his *Dictionnaire de Pédagogie*, pronounces the *Didactica Magna* "one of the most remarkable treatises that have been written on the science of education".

II. Janua Linguarum Reserata

This work, published at Lissa in 1631, was suggested by a book bearing the same title, written by an Irish Jesuit named Batty, who was connected with the Jesuit College at Salamanca. It was translated, as Comenius himself tells us, into Greek, Bohemian, Polish, Swedish, Belgian, English, French, Spanish, Italian, Hungarian, Turkish, Arabic, Persian, and even Mongolic. The general plan of the Janua may be seen from the following quotation: "Comenius believed that the knowledge of words should serve at the same time to acquire a knowledge of things. He therefore resolved to classify in methodical order all created things, with their Latin names, and a translation, in parallel columns; and to make of this general vocabulary a universal repertory of information, where the pupil might at the same time learn Latin and general science. He collected eight thousand words, with which he constructed one thousand sentences, and these he distributed into one hundred chapters."

III. Orbis Sensualium Pictus, *hoc est, omnium fundamentalium in mundo rerum, et in vita actionum, pictura et nomenclatura.*

The first edition of this famous book was published at Nuremberg in 1657; and soon after a translation was made into English by Charles Hoole. The last English edition appeared in 1777, and this was reprinted in America in 1812. A fine reprint of the English edition of 1727, with reproduction of the 151 copper-cut illustrations of the original edition of

1658, was published by C. W. Bardeen, Syracuse, in 1887.

This was the first illustrated school-book, and was the first attempt at what now passes under the name of "object lessons".

"The 'Orbis' was, in substance, the same as the 'Janua', though abbreviated, but it had this distinctive feature, that each subject was illustrated by a small engraving, in which everything named in the letter press below was marked with a number, and its name was found connected with the same number in the text."—*Quick*.

Educational Principles of Comenius

(Arranged from Paroz's Historie Universelle de la Pédagogie.)

1. Instruction is easy in proportion as it follows the course of nature.

2. Instruction ought to be progressive and adapted to the growing vigor of the intellectual faculties.

3. It is a fundamental error to begin instruction with languages and terminate it with things—mathematics, natural history, etc.; for things are the substance, the body, while words are the accident, the dress. These two portions of knowledge should be united, but we should begin with things, which are the objects of thought and of speech.

4. It is also an error to begin the study of language with grammar. We should first present the subject matter in an author or a well-arranged vocabulary. The form, *i. e.* the grammar, does not come till afterwards.

5. We should first exercise the senses (perception), then the memory, then the intelligence, and lastly the judgment (reasoning). For science begins with the observation; the impressions received are then imprinted upon the memory and the imagination; the intelligence next seizes upon the notions held in store in the memory and from them deduces general ideas; finally the reason draws conclusions from the things sufficiently known and co-ordinated in the intelligence.

6. It is not sufficient, merely to make the pupil comprehend; he should also learn to express and to apply what he has comprehended.

7. It is not the shadow of things which impresses the senses and the imagination, but the things themselves. It is then by a real intuition that instruction should begin, and not by a verbal description of things.

8. By observation, the pupil should first gain a general notion of an object, and should then observe each part by itself and in its relation to the whole.

9. Talent is developed by exercise. We learn to write by writing, to sing by singing, etc.

10. The study of languages ought to commence with the mother tongue. A language is learned better by use, by the ear, by writing, etc., than by rules, which should follow use in order to give it greater exactness.

—— *THE SCHOOL BULLETIN PUBLICATIONS.* ——

History of Modern Education.

The History of Modern Education. An account of Educational Opinion and Practice from the Revival of Learning to the Present Decade. By SAMUEL G. WILLIAMS, Ph.D., Professor of the Science and Art of Teaching in Cornell University. Cloth, 16mo, pp. 499. With 37 Portraits. $1.50.

This is a revised and enlarged edition of what was upon its first appearance altogether the fullest and most complete history of modern education now available. It is the only adequate preparation for examinations, and a necessary part of every teacher's working library.

The titles of the chapters will give some idea of its comprehensiveness. Those in italics appear for the first time in this revised edition.

Introductory. Valuable contributions to pedagogy from ancient days. I. Preliminaries of modern education. II. The Renaissance, and some interesting phases of education in the 16th century. III. Educational opinions of the 16th century. IV. Distinguished teachers of the 16th century, Melanchthon, Sturm, Trotzendorf, Neander, Ascham, Mulcaster, the Jesuits. V. Some characteristics of education in the 17th century. VI. Principles of the educational reformers. VII. The 17th century reformers. VIII. Female education and Fenelon. IX. The Oratory of Jesus. Beginnings of American education. X. Characteristics of education in the 18th century. XI. Important educational treatises of the 18th century: Rollin, Rousseau, Kant. XII. Basedow and the Philanthropinic experiment. XIII. Pestalozzi and his work. XIV. General review of education in the 18th century. XV. Educational characteristics of the 19th century. XVI. *Extension of popular education.* XVII. *Froebel and the kindergarten.* XVIII. *Professional training of teachers, and school supervision.* XIX. *Manual and industrial training.* XX. *Improvements in methods of instruction.* XXI. *Discussion of relative value of studies.*

There are also added an Analytic Appendix, for review; the Syllabus on the History of Education prepared by the Department of Public Instruction for the training classes of the State of New York, with references by page to this volume; and an Index of 13 double column pages, much fuller than in the first edition.

The *Critic* calls it, "sensible in its views, and correct and clear in style." The *American Journal of Education* says: "It is not too much to say that for all ordinary purposes Prof. Williams's book is in itself a much more valuable pedagogical library than could be formed with it omitted."

C. W. BARDEEN, Publisher, Syracuse, N. Y.

——— *THE SCHOOL BULLETIN PUBLICATIONS.* ———

Helps in the History of Education

1. *Essays on Educational Reformers.* By ROBERT HENRY QUICK. 16mo, pp. 429. Manilla 50 cts.; Cloth $1.00.

"With the suggestion that *study should be made interesting,*" wrote General Morgan, when principal of the Rhode Island State Normal School, "we most heartily agree. How this may be done, the attentive reader will be helped in learning by the study of this admirable book." The American Library Association recognize its literary value by including our edition of it in their list published by the Bureau of Education of books that every public library should own. An entirely new *illustrated* edition has now been issued, with autobiography, chapter on Froebel, 21 portraits, and 13 illustrations.

2. *Lectures on the History of Education in Prussia and England.* By JAMES DONALDSON. Cloth, 12mo, pp. 185. $1.00.

3. *A Short History of Education.* By Chancellor W. H. PAYNE. Cloth, 16mo, pp. 105. 50 cts.

This is a reprint of Oscar Browning's article in the Encyclopædia Britannica, with notes on Comenius and Bibliography.

4. *Sketches from the History of Education.* By W. N. HAILMANN. Paper, 8vo, pp. 39. 20 cts.

This treats particularly of Luther, Bacon, Pestalozzi, Girard, Diesterweg, and Froebel.

5. *History of the Philosophy of Pedagogics.* By Prof. C. W. BENNETT. Leatherette, 16mo, pp. 43. 50 cts.

6. *Elementary Greek Education.* By FRED H. LANE. Leatherette, 16mo, pp. 85. 50 cts.

7. *History of the Burgh Schools of Scotland.* By JAMES GRANT. Cloth, 8vo, pp. 571. $3.00. These were the original free schools of the world.

8. *The History of the High School of Edinburgh.* By WILLIAM STEVEN. Cloth, 12mo, pp. 610. $2.00.

9. *History of the Schools of Syracuse, N. Y.* By EDWARD SMITH. Cloth, 8vo, gilt top, pp. 347. With 85 portraits and 30 pictures of buildings. $3.00.

10. *Teachers' Institutes, Past and Present.* By JAMES M. MILNE. Paper, 8vo, pp. 22. 25 cts.

11. *History of Educational Journalism in the State of New York.* By C. W. BARDEEN. Paper, 8vo, pp. 45. 40 cts.

12. *Educational Publications in Italy.* By PIERO BARBERA. Paper, 8vo, pp. 14. 15 cts. Written for the Columbian Exposition.

C. W. BARDEEN, Publisher, Syracuse, N. Y.

―――*THE SCHOOL BULLETIN PUBLICATIONS.*―――

Meiklejohn's Life of Andrew Bell.

An old Educational Reformer, Dr. Andrew Bell. By J. M. D. MEIKLEJOHN, professor of the theory, history, and practice of education in the university of St. Andrews. Cloth, 16mo, pp. 182. $1.00.

Teachers of this generation can hardly realize what a power the monitorial system was in the history of the first third of this century. It was the subject most debated when teachers met together and in the educational journals of the time. It was supposed to have revolutionized teaching, and in this country as well as in England and elsewhere its influence was enormous. Dr. Andrew Bell, its founder is buried in Westminster Abbey, his tablet being one of the first that meets the eye of the visitor. He left a fortune of a million dollars to educational uses, and founded the chairs of education in the universities of Edinburgh and St. Andrews.

Hitherto his biography could be obtained only in the three enormous volumes of 2,000 pages by Robert Southey; but Dr. Meiklejohn, who occupies at St. Andrews the chair Dr. Bell founded, has written this memoir, which is as sprightly and interesting as the big compilation of Southey's is dreary and dull. He tells of Dr. Bell's college life, of his going to Virginia to be a tutor; of his shipwreck on his return voyage; of the duel he fought, when, being short-sighted and excitable, he fired at the seconds instead of his opponent; of his being offered $2,500 to vote for one candidate and immediately voting for the other; of his journey to India, where he was put in charge of an orphan school for boys; of his difficulty in finding teachers, and his discovery of the plan of mutual instruction; of the enormous success that this plan met with, first in India, and afterward in Great Britain and throughout the world.

Incidentally Prof. Meiklejohn tells much of the state of education at the time Dr. Bell began to introduce his system, when in Ireland for instance, the boy who had written the best copy was ordered by the master to pull the hair of the boy who had written the worst, and so to do until they arrived at their seats in the school again. It was one of Dr. Bell's correspondents who speaks of the death of a schoolmaster in Swabia who had superintended a seminary 51 years with severity; had given 911,500 canings, 124,000 floggings, 209,000 custodies, 136,000 tips with the ruler, 10,200 boxes on the ear, 22,700 tasks by heart, 700 stands upon peas, 600 kneels on a sharp edge, 500 foolscaps, 1,700 holds of rods.

In short the volume is a vivacious and interesting history of the time, as well as the best biography of one of England's most eminent teachers.

C. W. BARDEEN, Publisher, Syracuse, N. Y.

Biographies of Great Teachers.

1. *A Memoir of Roger Ascham*, by SAMUEL JOHNSON, LL.D.; and selections from the *Life of Thomas Arnold*, by Dean STANLEY. Edited, with Introductions and Notes by JAMES S. CARLISLE. 16mo, pp. 272. Manilla, 50 cts.; Cloth, $1.00.

THOMAS ARNOLD.

Besides the biography of Ascham in full this volume contains selections from "The Schoolmaster", with facsimile of the ancient title-page. We also publish Ascham's Complete Works in four handsome volumes at $5.00.

From Stanley's "Life of Arnold" those chapters have been taken which refer to his work as a teacher, and are published without change. Thus the book gives in full compass and at a low price all that is most important in the lives of these two great teachers.

"No better reading could be selected for the teacher, none more stimulating, none more softening, than the lives of these two men, so conspicuous for their achievement as teachers."—*The Evangelist*.

2. *John Amos Comenius, Bishop of the Moravians; his Life and Educational Works*. By S. S. LAURIE. 16mo, pp. 232. Manilla, 50 cts.; Cloth, $1.

3. *An Old Educational Reformer. Dr. Andrew Bell*. By J. M. D. MEIKLEJOHN. Cloth, 16mo, pp. 182. $1.00.

Dr. Bell was the founder of the Monitorial System that swept over England and America in the early part of this century, and was at that time the most famous teacher in the world. Prof. Meiklejohn has made his biography as entertaining as it is important in the history of education.

4. *Pestalozzi; his Aim and Work*. By Baron DEGUIMPS. Translated by MARGARET CUTHBERTSON CROMBIE. Cloth, 12mo, pp. 336. $1.50.

5. *Autobiography of Frederich Frœbel*. Translated and annotated by EMILIE MICHAELIS and H. KEATLEY MOORE. Cloth, 12mo, pp. 183. $1.50.

"He writes so simply and confidentially that no one can fail to understand everything in this new translation. It would be of great benefit to American youth for fathers and mothers to read this book for themselves, instead of leaving it entirely to professional teachers."—*New York Herald*.

6. *The Educational Labors of Henry Barnard*. By WILL S. MONROE. Leatherette, 16mo, pp. 35. 50 cts.

7. *Essays on Educational Reformers*. By R. H. QUICK. Cloth, 16mo, pp. 331. $1.50.

Its vivacious style makes it the most interesting of educational histories. We publish separately at 15 cts. each these chapters: I. The Jesuits, II. Comenius, III. Locke, IV. Rousseau, V. Basedow, VI. Jacotot, VII. Pestalozzi.

C. W. BARDEEN, Publisher, Syracuse, N. Y.

www.ingramcontent.com/pod-product-compliance
Lightning Source LLC
Chambersburg PA
CBHW032242080426
42735CB00008B/964